The land of the setting sun

JEREMY HARTLEY/OXFAM

THE LAND OF THE SETTING SUN, African travellers used to call it, when they reached the westernmost tip of their vast continent and gazed out over the Atlantic Ocean. They came as pioneers from the east and the north, to a place where cool sea breezes met and mingled with hot dry winds from the Sahara.

From the tenth century onwards, waves of migration brought settlers to this land. Their cultures met and merged, creating an intricate pattern of currents that makes up the rich inner life and spirit of the people of Senegal. The rise and fall of kingdoms and principalities brought wealth and power to one ethnic group after another. The people were exposed successively to the great empire of Mali, to the Arab civilisation of North Africa, and to the Europe of merchants, missionaries, and slave-traders. Each has helped to shape the country's culture and customs.

In the past 150 years, Islam has swept through Senegal. Some ruling families and traders had adopted the religion of Mohammed centuries earlier, but today nine out ten Senegalese are Muslim; the rest are Christian or animist, in roughly equal numbers. But for most Senegalese, these monotheist creeds are not incompatible with the beliefs of their traditional religions, which they have not abandoned.

Perhaps the temperate trade winds have something to do with the reputation of the Wolof, the country's largest ethnic group, for being cool-headed and tolerant. Whatever the reasons, Senegal has the best human-rights record in Africa, as measured by the Human Freedoms Index of the UN Development Programme. On this index, Senegal ranks a few points behind Spain and Ireland. It was the first country in Africa to allow free rein to a political opposition. Freedom of speech and freedom of the press are now taken for granted.

These political freedoms have to be balanced against the fact that, barring unforeseen events, by the year 2000 the same party will have been in control of the presidential palace for 40 uninterrupted years, since Senegal gained independence from France. Some Senegalese grumble that their democratic institutions, much admired by the outside world, don't always live up to their reputation.

Along the river

Much of the history, ancient wealth, and spiritual foundations of Senegal originate in the wide curving swathe of land that follows the course of the Senegal River from the hilly region of the south-east to its mouth at the old capital of St Louis in the north-west. For many centuries the river was the people's principal artery of

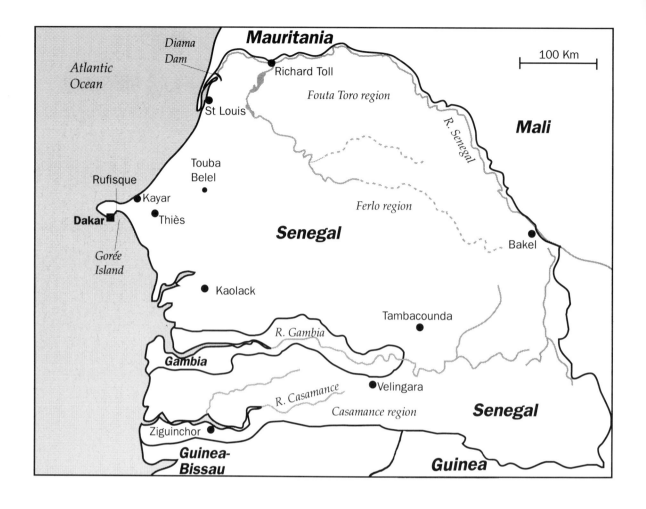

communication and trade; it also gave them a fertile strip of land for their crops, and water for the livestock which came down from their upland pastures in the dry season.

South and west from the river, the land quickly dries to a flat, sparsely wooded savannah, dotted here and there with the small villages of Peulh pastoralists, their thatched huts usually grouped around a well where their animals can be watered. Farther south, the thin cover of thorn bushes gives way to larger trees, and then to landscapes dominated by armies of majestic baobab trees, their arms outstretched like sentinels in a hundred strange poses. Here one is in the so-called 'peanut basin': the agricultural heartland which produces the largest share of the country's income. It is a huge zone, stretching from the region of Thiès in the west to Tambacounda in the east. After the annual harvest, the peanuts are gathered in great mountains to await transportation. But there are also sand dunes and abandoned fields where, after a few years of lucrative crops, nothing more will grow.

From the river to the Gambian border, Senegal is a dry land, most of it forming part of the Sahelian arid zone that stretches from the Atlantic to the Red Sea. By contrast, the Casamance region in the south is the edge of a different world, bordering West Africa's forest region and receiving five times as much rain as the far north of the country. The Casamance has its own river, a luxuriant vegetation, and the very particular culture of its forest people, still somewhat sheltered from (or, as some complain, ignored by) the forces of modernisation.

Senegal

A State of Change

Contents

JEREMY HARTLEY/OXFAM

Designed by Oxfam Design Department
Published and printed by Oxfam,
274 Banbury Road, Oxford OX2 7DZ, UK
ISBN 0 85598 283 7
© Oxfam (UK & Ireland) 1994
Registered charity no. 202918

Robin Sharp

COLÁISTE MHU   1

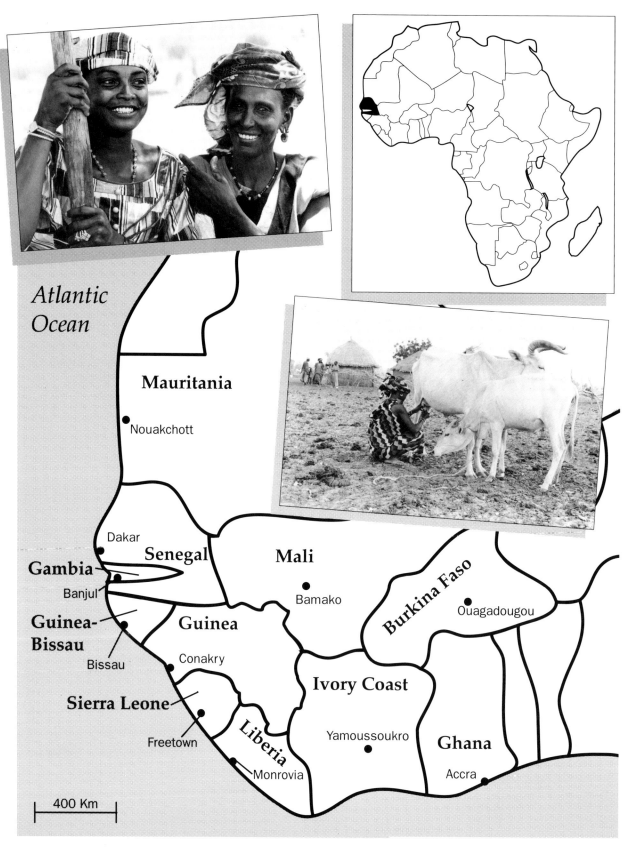

Atlantic
Ocean

Mauritania

• Nouakchott

Dakar
• **Senegal**   **Mali**

Gambia
Banjul   **Guinea**   Bamako

**Guinea-
Bissau**

Bissau   Conakry

Sierra Leone

Freetown

Burkina Faso

• Ouagadougou

Ivory Coast

Liberia   Yamoussoukro   **Ghana**

Monrovia   Accra

| 400 Km |

Times are getting harder

Senegal's rich history and culture should have stood the new nation in good stead when it became independent in 1960. The omens were promising. The capital, Dakar, was the established gateway for foreign trade with French West Africa, and the country had a relatively well-developed business and industrial sector, built up by the French to serve all their territories to the east.

These advantages began to fade, however, as neighbouring countries started to assert their own economic independence. Agricultural output was increasing, but world prices for African produce were falling. And for the past 20 years the problems of the new and fragile economy have been compounded by other adversities: a long and disastrous drought, the erosion of natural resources, and the inexorable noose of foreign debt. The result is that Senegal has seen its goal of economic independence receding year by year. Most people are actually worse off than they were in 1970.

In 1980, faced with the prospect of bankruptcy, the government of Senegal recognised the failures of its centrally planned economy, and became the first in sub-Saharan Africa to call in the World Bank and the International Monetary Fund to devise a rescue package. The price of that rescue was a Structural Adjustment Programme, based on the principles of free-market capitalism. Since 1984 the government has had to cut state services drastically, liquidating or selling off many government-run agencies, and making many public-sector workers redundant..

Some progress has been made towards balancing the country's income and expenditure, but for most people the reforms have only created more hardship. Disappearing government services have left a vacuum, especially in areas like technical support for agriculture. Crop yields have declined, and the result is a continuing exodus from the countryside. Tens of thousands abandon their rural homes every year to seek a living in the towns; up to half a million are now working abroad. Senegal faces challenges that are complex and daunting; but they must be faced squarely — not only by the Senegalese themselves, but by those in the rich industrialised countries whose policies contribute to the problems of poor people in Africa.

A short book like this cannot do justice to the vitality and diversity of Senegal. No book can convey the essential elements of life in this corner of West Africa: the music, the jokes, the aroma of fish and spices, the ready *bonhomie* between strangers. Times may be hard and getting harder, but the Senegalese have a knack of making the best of whatever fate throws at them.

Flower sellers in a Dakar market

Travellers from an antique land

I T IS AN IRONY OF HISTORY that the main ethnic groups of Senegal probably have their roots in a civilisation older than that of the Europeans who believed they had a 'mission to civilise' their colonial subjects. There is some evidence that they are descended from people who were part of the Pharaonic civilisation of ancient Egypt. In particular, the **Lébou**, who settled on the Dakar peninsula and are related to the now much more numerous **Wolof**, are believed by some to be the same Lébou who are recorded as being fishing people in the Red Sea and then, later, on the Mediterranean coast of present-day Libya.

One theory suggests that before 4000 BC the Lébou had reached Egypt from India. In any case, they and other groups — presumably farmers and cattle herders — journeyed across the continent in waves, eventually reaching the rich kingdom of Tokrour, in what is now Mauritania, around the tenth century AD, before moving south across the Senegal River.

Even so, an Iron Age civilisation had been there before them. There are many burial mounds and other neolithic sites scattered around the country. The road to Tambacounda, the capital of Senegal's Eastern Region, passes through the small village of Douba Lampo where, beside the road, among today's thatched huts, chickens are scratching and children playing around the ancient pillars of a megalithic stone circle. A few are broken, but most of the ironstone columns, rough but perfectly cylindrical, about five feet high, are still in place. Who built them remains a mystery.

As the Lébou and their fellow travellers migrated south from Mauritania, the **Mandingue** people from Mali who had occupied the centre of present-day Senegal were pushed into the southern part of the country, where they remain, along with the indigenous, forest-dwelling **Diola** of the Casamance.

The fourteenth and fifteenth centuries saw the rise of independent Senegalese kingdoms: the Djoloff empire of the Wolof in the west and centre; the Fouta of the already islamicised **Toucouleur** in the north; and the Gabu of the Mandingue south of the Gambia River. The Djoloff empire was broken up around 1550, by which time the first Portuguese explorers had reached the coast of Senegal and established trading posts. They were followed over the next 300 years by the Dutch, the French, and the British.

Megalithic stone circle at the village of Douba Lampo, near Koumpentoum

From slavery to independence

IN 1450, the first recorded European explorer landed on the coast of Senegal. The Venetian Alvise de Ca da Mosto, working for Prince Henry the Navigator of Portugal, was received by the king of Kayar, who ruled the coastal region. Neither of them knew it, but it was the start of five centuries of pillage of the country's wealth and its people.

At first, the Europeans were searching for gold or other precious metals — or, in the case of Henry, the chance to spread the Christian gospel. But soon a lucrative trade in human lives was under way, and by 1550 one-tenth of the population of Lisbon consisted of black slaves. Up to this point, the treatment of slaves was similar to the traditional African system, which usually made them members of the master's family and sometimes gave them considerable rights.

An abominable trade

The Portuguese dominated the West African coast until the mid-1500s, when the British and Dutch began to establish their own trading posts, followed by the French. The slave trade then changed gear. From their fortified trading camps on the coast, the Europeans offered alcohol, clothes, earrings, and other cheap goods, including old muskets and rifles, in exchange for gold, ivory and, above all, human cargoes. Slaves brought from the interior by their African captors were collected in warehouses. Most were peasants, captured and sold by the more warlike and better-organised tribes.

In the mid-1700s, the key trading posts on the Senegal coast changed hands several times between the warring British and French. In 1768, Britain proclaimed the establishment of the Crown Colony of

The slave trade commemorated in a street mural painted by young people in Dakar, 1990

A haunted island

Becalmed in a heat haze just two miles off Dakar's coast stands the little island which is perhaps Africa's most poignant place of pilgrimage. Gorée is a haunted isle: beautiful with its villas, sandy streets, palm trees, and bright splashes of bougainvillaea against a blue backdrop of sea and sky; but sorrowful with the silent echo of atrocities committed here through the centuries of the slave trade.

With a good harbour and protective cliffs, from the fifteenth century onwards Gorée was seen as an ideal fortress and depot by the Europeans, seeking to control their trade along the coast. It changed hands 15 times between the Portuguese, Dutch, English, and French before the French secured possession, and in the process — despite the grim trade being pursued in the slave houses — many of the local people prospered.

In 1780, more than half of the 18 villas on Gorée belonged to the aristocratic *Signares*, wealthy women of mixed African and European parentage, who made marriages of convenience with European administrators, officers, or merchants for the duration of their stay. And while the captives awaiting transportation languished in chains nearby, the fine houses of the island were the scene of elegant banquets and dances.

Today, the ferryboat from Dakar brings visitors from many countries. They come to the *Maison des Esclaves* (Slave House), some to meditate on their African roots, and some to reflect on the history of man's inhumanity to man.

Senegambia, its first colony in Africa. But it was not long before the French retook the coast north of the Gambia River. Throughout the eighteenth century, both countries were heavily engaged in the transatlantic slave trade.

At the slave houses, families were split up and babies taken from their mothers. Then the captives were sold and stamped with their owners' initials before being stacked head to toe in the boats for transportation as forced labour to the American colonies. Many died in chains on the voyage. Before arrival in the Americas, the sick were often thrown overboard, to avoid paying landing taxes on them.

This trade in human lives did not go unchallenged. In Britain, the abolitionist movement, started by Wilberforce and others, led to the banning of the colonial slave trade in 1807. But other countries were slower to renounce it. Slavery was not abolished in Senegal until 1848.

An estimated 10 million Africans were sold into the transatlantic slave trade, and many more were killed in battles to capture them, in long marches, in revolts,

or by suicide. Over four centuries, a total of 50 to 60 million lives were destroyed. In Senegal, as in other West African countries, this devastation is deeply seared into the nation's memory. Yet today there is rarely a trace of bitterness in the welcome given to people of white skin by the descendants of the slaves.

Colonisation

On the mainland of Senegal, the various kingdoms remained independent until the middle of the nineteenth century. In 1790, the Lébou of the Dakar peninsula won independence from Kayar, and the French garrison on the nearby island of Gorée had to deal with a well-organised and surprisingly democratic government. Under its president, the Lébou republic had a cabinet of ministers, an Assembly of Wise Men (Senate), and a House of Representatives with seats for each zone of the country.

The Lébou maintained generally cordial relations with the French and welcomed their missionaries — their first encounter with followers of Issa Ibnou

Mariam (Jesus Christ), whom they knew of from the Koran. In 1847, the head of French missions reported home that the Lébou had 'a purity of customs as great as Muslim polygamy allows. Their uprightness, probity, and respect for marriage, the obedience of children to their parents, their affection for their fathers and the hospitality of the Wolofs are in contrast with European behaviour. Murder, theft, and fraud are things unheard of here.'

Ten years later the French established a base on the Dakar mainland. Respecting the Lébou, for a time they still paid them fees and taxes; but gradually they annexed more and more land. Resistance to the French occupation was led by Lat-Dyor Diop, who at the age of 20 overthrew the French-protected King of Kayar and then for nearly 25 years waged guerrilla warfare against the invaders. Lat-Dyor is revered as one of the great heroes of Senegal's struggle for freedom. At the time of his death in 1886, however, France had gained control of all the territory of modern Senegal. The St Louis-Dakar railway, which Lat-Dyor had most bitterly opposed, was built, and also the Port of Dakar. The French seized land

rights from the traditional chiefs and introduced taxes, forcing the peasants into a money economy.

In the 1870s, inhabitants of France's four main settlements — Dakar, St Louis, Gorée, and Rufisque — were accorded the status of French citizens. The rest of the population were classed as 'subjects' — subject to forced labour, taxes, and passes required for travelling from one village to another. Schools were founded in which the pupils were required to speak French; national languages were banned. Thus the colonial power created a rootless elite, trained to manage their own people like good Frenchmen.

In 1902, Dakar became the capital of all French West Africa, a huge territory stretching 2,000 miles east to Lake Chad, while St Louis under its French Governor remained the capital of Senegal itself. Senegal was granted representation in the French National Assembly, and the first black MP, Blaise Diagne, elected in 1914, rose to be Under-Secretary of State for the Colonies. At the end of World War II, one of Senegal's seats was held by the future president, Léopold Senghor. Educated at a Parisian school in the same class as another

'Put the verbs in brackets into the future tense': French is the official language of Senegal — a legacy from the colonial era

9

future president, Georges Pompidou, Senghor became a professor of French. He helped to develop the concept of *négritude,* to restore African dignity after the centuries of slavery and colonial exploitation. *Négritude* extolled the values of black culture, especially its communal spirit, its warmth and spontaneity, its sense of rhythm, and its mystical elements — all in contrast with European rationalism.

Independence

Before independence, Senghor campaigned for a federation of French African states, and opposed the fragmentation of the continent. But other African leaders with narrow, territorialist ambitions wanted their own personal slice of the cake, and Senghor's appeal for unity went unheeded. An attempted federation with Mali in 1960, the year of independence, came unstuck, so Senghor became the President of Senegal, as he was to remain for the next 20 years. Three times he was re-elected as the candidate of the only political party, the Parti Socialiste, on a platform proclaiming 'African socialism'. Before the election of 1978, two opposition parties had been allowed to form — the only case in this period of an African government voluntarily ending the one-party system — but Senghor won again. Two years later, as he called in the World Bank and the IMF to save his failing economy, Senghor retired and handed over the presidency to his chosen heir, the tall, reserved technocrat, Abdou Diouf.

Three elections later, Diouf is still there, and meanwhile has opened up the political field by abolishing most restrictions on the formation of new parties. As a result, there are now at least 17, though the ruling Socialists and the main opposition group, the Senegalese Democratic Party of Maitre Abdoulaye Wade, leave the rest out of sight. Opposition charges of electoral fraud after Diouf was declared the winner of the 1988 election led to several months of rioting and strikes. The government subsequently agreed to introduce a new electoral code, worked out in consultation with the opposition, to rule out the possibility of vote-rigging. Although Diouf won again in 1993, the result was accepted this time without any serious unrest.

A man of many cultures

The three cultures of his ancestors — Serer, Mandinka, and Peulh— were not enough for Léopold Sédar Senghor. In 1928, after attending a Catholic school in Senegal, he went to France to pursue his studies and in due course became the first African qualified to teach in a French *lycée* (high school).

After World War II, during which he was imprisoned by the Germans for opposing their occupation of France, Senghor was elected to the French National Assembly. Fifteen years later, renowned as a poet and intellectual as well as a politician, he became President of his newly-independent country.

Immersed in French academic and political life, but determined to reassert the values of African culture, Senghor happily described himself as 'a cultural half-caste'. He espoused the idea of 'universal civilisation' — a concept that was light years away from the concerns of his compatriots— and yet, by force of personality and some canny manoeuvring, he managed to retain their support and affection.

Senghor was a man of many parts. He could talk of ecology or economics, anthropology or exchange rates, and his leadership gave Senegal a respected voice on the international stage. His retirement in 1980 permitted a peaceful transfer of power, without any of the violence or military interference which have blighted other countries of the region.

Dakar: signs of a free press are everywhere

St Louis: election posters, 1993. President Diouf's Socialist Party won, with a reduced majority of 70 seats; the Democratic Party, the main opposition group, won 40 of the 120 assembly seats.

Nationhood:
a false start

THE FIRST YEARS OF NATIONHOOD seemed to be going well enough, but after 1968 the chickens of misguided policy and bad advice from abroad started coming home to roost. The few critics who saw them coming argued against development policies which favoured the rich and the town-dwellers at the expense of the peasants. But the governments of Senegal and other Sahelian countries soon had more convenient explanations for why things were going wrong: a disastrous drought and worsening terms of trade for their exports on world markets.

The long drought ...

The rains, on which life and livelihoods depend in the Sahelian zone, had been abundant in the 1950s and early 1960s. Then in 1968 they failed, heralding the drought which struck the whole Sahel two years later and which has continued, with some years of remission, for more than 20 years. The drought has destroyed whole communities and forced large numbers of people to abandon their land and become economic refugees in search of something to eat. In 1992, while most of the Sahel had good crops, much of northern and central Senegal once again suffered drought.

Only 40 per cent of Senegal's land area now receives more than 600mm of rain a year, compared with 60 per cent at the time of independence. Wells in many parts of the country have run dry as the water table has sunk. The flow of rivers has dropped dramatically, threatening agriculture and fishing as sea water invades the estuaries.

The rains — normally concentrated in the months from June to October — have also become extremely erratic. This lends circumstantial support to the theory, as yet unproven, that the Sahel is already a victim of global warming, provoked by the car exhausts, chemicals, and industries of 'developed' countries in the North.

... and a top-heavy State

The drought, though devastating, is not enough to explain Senegal's downward economic spiral. Other factors were at work too. It didn't help that the over-valued currency encouraged non-essential imports and made Senegalese products too expensive to be competitive in foreign markets. Nor that the government, encouraged by foreign financiers and international aid agencies, was accumulating debts to pay for grandiose and unproductive development projects. Nor that most of the nation's disposable wealth settled in the hands of the rich and powerful, who put short-term gains before national investment and growth. Meanwhile the peasants, who should have been producing a large share of the nation's wealth, were getting progressively poorer.

A deserted village near Loumbol, abandoned during the drought in 1991. The village well, already 70 metres deep, had dried up and could not be deepened.

JEREMY HARTLEY/OXFAM

A huge parastatal development agency — ONCAD — was set up in 1966 and soon took over management of the whole agricultural system. ONCAD was supposed to train rural co-operatives, manage the supply of farm inputs (seeds, pesticides, and machines), and oversee the work of four separate agencies for rice, peanuts, cotton, and livestock. It quickly became a bureaucratic monster, consuming the resources it was supposed to administer, and leaving farmers with little incentive to improve their productive capacity. In 1980 ONCAD was finally put into liquidation with a deficit of nearly £200 million.

Austerity begins to bite

Senegal's rural communities hoped for something better after the collapse of ONCAD. But the 1980s brought even greater upheaval, as the austerity measures and drastic reforms demanded by the World Bank and IMF began to bite. Under the New Agricultural Policy of 1984, farm subsidies were abolished and the government suddenly stopped providing the seeds, fertilisers, and support services on which farmers had come to depend. The idea was to hand over all these things to the private sector, but nobody was prepared for the change — least of all the peasants. It was not so much 'structural adjustment' as major surgery without any anaesthetic. A new bank for rural credit was set up, but again without consulting the people for whom it was intended. Farmers, fishing people, and pastoralists all protest that its terms are too rigid and beyond their means. So, being unable to invest, they suffer another twist in the spiral of decline.

Despite rapid urbanisation, most Senegalese still depend on the rural economy for their living. Yet the value of farm produce going to market has fallen by a third since the 1960s. For a variety of reasons — lack of help with credit and marketing, falling productivity, and having more mouths to feed — farmers are switching back to their traditional subsistence crops, simply for survival. As a consequence they have less and less to sell to feed the towns. This in turn means ever-increasing food imports, and therefore ever-increasing debt. For a government which proclaimed food self-sufficiency to be its most important goal, today's reality is a trend towards greater dependency that will be extremely difficult to break.

In the towns and cities, output in the fragile industrial sector has suffered from high costs and an exchange rate which was estimated to overvalue the CFA franc in Senegal by at least 40 per cent. Factories have closed, foreign investors are staying away, and unemployment is running at 20 per cent or more.

President Diouf and his team have engaged in an elaborate game of shadow boxing with the World Bank to delay and modify the reforms demanded of them. They may have had good reason to resist some of them, but the net effect is that the overwhelming burden of adjustment from a centrally-planned to a free-market economy is being borne by poor people in the towns and countryside.

JEREMY HARTLEY/OXFAM

Coping with crisis ... sénégalaisement

Desperate remedies

As the State withdraws from many sectors of the economy, the people of Senegal have realised that they must sink or swim. Their former livelihoods or support systems have been swept away, but many have been quick to find alternative ways to survive. While a quarter of Dakar's workforce is unemployed, the number of working women doubled in the three years to 1991. The informal economy of small traders, artisans, caterers, and a hundred other mini-businesses has mushroomed. At this level there is no shortage of ingenuity, with flattened beer cans recycled to make an original line in attaché cases, and scraps of cloth reworked into fashionable patchwork clothes.

Now, as formal jobs run out, many educated people are also being forced into self-employment. Young men with cassette recorders make pirate tapes of pop music to sell on the street; phone and fax bureaux are sprouting in provincial centres; and elegantly dressed women jet back and forth to Europe and the United States, running their own import-export businesses dealing in clothes, cosmetics, and household goods. With Senegal's high import duties, there's also plenty of profit for those smuggling in cheap goods from neighbouring countries.

Spending and saving

If they have it, the Senegalese do enjoy spending money and showing off what they've got. But they can also be diligent savers, whether in cash or in kind. Pastoralists, who prefer to increase their herds rather than selling off animals for profit, are effectively building their savings on the hoof. Many town-dwellers have managed to save up for the down-payment for a house under the government's mortgage scheme.

Two forms of saving, neither yielding any interest, are popular throughout Senegal. These are the community chest and the *tontine*. The community chest is a form of social security fund. Each person or family head makes a regular contribution, and the fund is managed by a committee which gives grants to any members judged to be in need: to meet the costs of urgent medical treatment or funeral expenses, for instance.

The informal economy in action: a tannery in Pikine, on the outskirts of Dakar

JEREMY HARTLEY/OXFAM

Diadou makes ends meet

In a suburb of Ziguinchor, capital of the Casamance region, Diadou, a dressmaker in her mid-twenties, contributes 1,500 CFA francs a month to her husband's Village Association. Better off than most, she also gives 1,000 francs a month towards the building of a maternity unit in the village, and up to 500 francs whenever there's a baptism or marriage in the neighbourhood, so that the women can make a collective gift to the family concerned. Diadou also belongs to two *tontines*: one yields her 3,500 francs every seven weeks, with which she buys clothes for her children and household supplies such as cooking oil and petrol; the other, for a contribution of 500 francs a week, gives her 6,000 francs every three months, which she uses to buy needles, thread, and other supplies for her work.

The *tontine* is a kind of short-term insurance scheme, in which a group of friends or colleagues agree to save so much a week each. It may be 100 CFA francs (equivalent to about 12 pence) or, in a few cases, several pounds. The contributions are held by a treasurer, and the total weekly or monthly income goes to each member in turn.

Most *tontines* have fewer than 10 members, who are chosen on the basis of personal trust and financial soundness. Usually they have no written statutes, and many never hold meetings. Occasionally someone runs off with the money, as happens in financial institutions everywhere, but in general they work well. The fact that they are informal, encourage togetherness, and can cope with very modest savings makes them worth more to most people than the few per cent interest they might get on a bank savings account.

When it comes to seeking credit, banks — with their strict repayment terms and often intimidating paperwork — are not widely used Many prefer to go to local money-lenders, often regarded by outsiders as 'exploiters of the poor'. In fact, though his interest rates will be higher than the bank's, the local money-lender shares more of the risk with the borrower. If your crops fail one year, he will normally agree to defer repayments; if a member of your family falls sick, he is probably the one with a vehicle who will give you transport to the nearest hospital.

These are some of the ways in which people are coping with crisis. For those without means of their own, there is still (unless they are very unlucky) the safety-net of the extended family.

In a slum quarter of central Dakar, a visitor stops to greet an old man with a deeply lined face who is walking slowly back to his tin shack. The visitor asks how he is faring and gets the standard, wry response of people who are getting by somehow, against all the odds.

OK, replies the old man with a shrug and a grin. '*Ça va, ça va ... sénégalaisement.*'

JEREMY HARTLEY/OXFAM

Making clothes in a Dakar market

Magicians, missionaries, and marabouts

A religion of the earth

When Africa's own gods ruled the lives of its people, the earth was revered as the source of life, to be held as a sacred trust for future generations. Traditional or 'animist' beliefs defined the spiritual context of people's lives, and conditioned their relations with the land and their environment. For the animist, all things, animate or otherwise, have a soul.

But it was an unequal struggle when this religion of the earth and the elements was challenged by gods from the north who had prophets in human form and books that proclaimed theirs to be the one true path. Missionaries of Islam and Christianity insisted on the superiority of their reading-and-writing religions: theirs was the power of the word.

Religions of the written word

Islam came to Senegal with evangelical warriors from the Arab kingdoms of North Africa, charging south across the Sahara and through present-day Mauritania. Christianity sailed in from the Atlantic with Europe's merchants, slave traders, and colonial armies.

Crossing the Senegal River in the fifteenth century, Islam spread gradually through the ruling families of the various kingdoms, usually as a result of trade or conquest. It was not adopted by the masses, however, until the nineteenth century, when there was much forced but superficial conversion. Since then, it has become firmly implanted as the guiding force of the nation's spiritual life. It also brought new ideas of personal and social behaviour, including habits of cleanliness, courtesy, and propriety. And it resulted in a rich and unique fusion of Berber, Arab, and Negro cultures, to which have been added more recent European influences.

Nominally, the country is now 90 per cent Muslim, with animism mostly confined to the Diola people of the Casamance. But that is less than half the truth. People often adopted Islam because it was compatible with — or prepared at least to condone — many of their traditional practices. In fact, Islam has some animist beliefs of its own, and its clerics or *marabouts* are not members of a priestly hierarchy. Islamic magicians, like their animist counterparts, make charms and amulets, often containing verses from the Koran or magic formulas and, even in the most islamicised region along the Senegal River, the traditional medicine man still functions as exorcist, rain-maker, diviner, and herbalist. Much of village life is still shaped by traditional religious practices.

This helps to explain why Senegal has developed its own liberal form of Islam, tolerant of other beliefs and other ways of life — and why women are subject to fewer restrictions on their freedom than in some Muslim societies. Practices vary

Thierno Sidig Hamedou Kane, a marabout, teaching the Koran to children in Dakar

between the towns and rural areas, but women generally are able to farm, travel, and conduct business on their own account. Much of the small-scale commerce of Senegal is in the hands of women entrepreneurs.

Christianity encountered strong resistance in Senegal, because it was associated with the colonial invaders, and because it made few concessions to the people's traditional beliefs. Today, the small Christian minority of Roman Catholics is found mostly in the regions of Dakar, Thiès, and the Casamance, where French missionaries arrived before Islam became entrenched. In these areas, traditional forms of social organisation have been modified in some significant ways (for example, by the acceptance of monogamy). Nevertheless, it is hard to gauge how deeply Christian beliefs and practices have taken root.

The power of the Islamic brotherhoods

One particular feature of Islam in Senegal are the *marabouts*, who have a unique role as wise men, teachers, priests, and mystics — as well as being, very often, semi-feudal landlords or affluent businessmen in rich robes and impenetrable dark glasses. During the colonial period, the French used their dealings with the business-like *marabouts* to weaken the authority of the traditional chiefs. At the same time, Islam was attracting more followers, as it became a force for national resistance to the colonial occupation and the alien values it had imposed.

With the growth of the new religion came the Islamic brotherhoods, as the faithful declared themselves followers of particular teachers. The Tidianes, probably still the most numerous in Senegal, follow the teachings of an Algerian holy man of the nineteenth century. Other fraternities are the Khadria, which started in Mauritania, and the Layènes around Dakar. But by far the greatest impact of the last 100 years, in terms of religious fervour, political influence, and commercial power, has been that of the Mourides.

Founded in about 1880 by the religious leader Cheikh Amadou Bamba, a fierce opponent of French rule, the Mouride brotherhood grew rapidly, especially among the Wolof, to its present numbers of more than one million. One of the principal tenets of Mouridisme is the redemptive power of work, and their leaders organised collective farm settlements which ran counter to the traditional pattern of family working units. As a result, they were in a position to convert small-scale peanut farming into an organised industry, encouraged by the French who, having expropriated all land rights, assigned large tracts to Mouride landowners, whose crops they then bought for processing into peanut oil. It was a convenient replacement for the outlawed slave trade.

Around the shrine of their founder, the town of Touba has grown into a holy city with one of Africa's most splendid mosques, attracting hundreds of thousands for the annual pilgrimage. Many of the rural faithful have accepted without question their obligation to work as sharecroppers for their *marabouts* or to give them a day's weekly labour; in the towns, they contribute a share of their cash income. Others, in their poverty, have had no option but to give themselves or their children, body and soul, to the *marabout*, on whom they depend for material as well as spiritual salvation. Some may be sent into the street to beg alms for their *marabout* and for their own meagre subsistence. Whatever its strengths and weaknesses, Mouridisme has been a dramatic force for change in Senegalese life. It has also won followers as far afield as the Caribbean and the United States.

One question for the future is whether the ever-harsher conditions of life for most Senegalese, contrasted with the affluent lifestyles of the elite in Dakar, may give rise to the kind of Islamic fundamentalism which has sown discord and violence in Sudan and parts of North Africa. In recent years there has been some evidence of incipient fundamentalism, not yet significant, but not something to be discounted.

The economy in a nutshell

The problem with peanuts

Senegal is stuck with its peanut economy, which employs over one million people, occupies 40 per cent of all cultivated land, and provides nearly half the country's export income. The Portuguese introduced peanuts into Senegal from Brazil in the sixteenth century; but it was the French who vastly expanded their cultivation as a cash crop for the market back home.

While it brings in much-needed foreign exchange, the modest peanut is now playing havoc with Senegal's financial and natural resources. In one recent year it cost the government 30 billion francs (about £60 million) to make up the difference between falling world prices and the price which it guarantees to farmers. And the methods of cultivation have degraded wide tracts of land, some now reduced to drifting sand, unable to support plant life. Peanuts, which grow underground, are harvested by digging up the whole plant, leaving the soil loose and exposed to erosion by wind or rain (unlike cereal crops, which leave roots and stubble behind to hold the soil together). The USA and Asian countries have been able to offset lower market prices by higher productivity on the same area of land, but output per hectare in Senegal's peanut basin has been stagnant, and the area planted to this crop has tended to decline.

The harsh reality is that the six out of every ten Senegalese who depend on rural livelihoods have, for the past 15 years, suffered an annual decline of 4.6 per cent in their real cash incomes. Farmers cannot afford to observe the recommended rotation of crops, leaving land fallow to

Peanut mountain at a state-owned mill near Kaolack. When crop yields are high, world prices for peanut oil fall. Badly stored peanuts can develop aflatoxin, a poisonous mould.

Fishing boats beached near Dakar. They look sturdy, but are easily smashed in collisions with industrial trawlers from Europe and Korea

restore its nutrients, with the result that there has been a general decline of 3-5 per cent a year in soil productivity.

More imports, fewer exports

Similar economic problems affect the main ingredients of Senegal's national dish, *tiep-bou-dien*: fish with rice. The fishing industry, besides supplying local markets, is the country's second biggest export-earner. In recent years new and more efficient nets and tackle, together with outboard motors, have increased the capacity of the country's fleet of inshore fishing *pirogues* — large canoes up to 12 metres long. But to pay for this new equipment, the small-scale fishermen have to land more fish to pay off their loans. Together with suspected over-fishing by European industrial trawlers in Senegalese waters, this means that fish stocks are now declining.

As for rice, farmers in the paddy fields along the Senegal River and in the Casamance cannot compete on price with their counterparts in South-East Asia. And, even with subsidies, they cannot produce half what the country consumes, so that means another large import bill.

But there's less money to pay it, since other farm exports such as tomatoes, peppers, green beans, and melons have fallen steadily since the early 1980s. They have been losing their share of the European market, owing to problems with air-freight transport and competition from Spain, Kenya, and Egypt.

On the industrial front, earnings from phosphate mining are growing, but they account for only a small share of export income, and other manufactured products contribute little. The New Industrial Policy (NIP), introduced in the mid-1980s as part of the structural adjustment programme, has frozen the national minimum wage and liberalised the job market, giving employers more scope to hire and fire staff. Under pressure from the World Bank, the NIP was also designed to reduce the tariffs which protected Senegalese industries from foreign competition — something that will be accentuated now that the Uruguay Round of the General Agreement on Tariffs and Trade has been finally concluded.

In common with nearly all African countries, Senegal's terms of trade — the prices it can obtain for its exports,

compared with what it has to pay for imports — have deteriorated seriously over the past decade, as world markets for primary commodities have slumped. Most of the country's peanut crop is sold for processing into oil; in one year (1985-86) the wholesale price of unrefined peanut oil crashed from over US$1,000 a ton to below $550 — an extreme example of how unstable markets can affect primary producers.

The Uruguay Round, concluded in December 1993, is essentially a package designed by the European Union and the USA. It is intended to widen access to world markets for all states, but one net result will be to give the more industrially advanced countries *carte blanche* to swamp Senegal and the rest of the developing world with cheap imports. This will make it virtually impossible for many of them to develop a viable manufacturing sector of their own.

Deepening debt and the risks of devaluation

Overhanging the economy, meanwhile, and severely constraining Senegal's room for economic manoeuvre, is a foreign debt which at the beginning of 1992 stood at $3.5 billion, according to the World Bank.

By the time the government has met its debt-service obligations, which swallow 30 per cent of all tax revenues, and paid public-sector salaries, which take another 58 per cent, there is precious little left to pay for schools, health services, housing, roads, or other operational expenses.

The overvalued CFA franc, tied at an unvarying rate to the French franc since 1948, made Senegal's exports more and more uncompetitive on the world market. Finally in January 1994, the CFA was devalued by 50 per cent against the French franc. Fortunately all countries in the region agreed to devalue by the same amount, so — at least for the time being — there is no danger that they will erect trade barriers against each other.

The currency remains linked to the French franc, but now it costs the Senegalese twice as much to buy it, and over twice as much to buy US dollars and some other currencies. In the import-dependent towns and cities, this came as a major shock, as almost all imported goods immediately doubled in price, and ordinary people's buying power was drastically reduced.

The theoretical benefits of the devaluation will not be seen for some time, but the government is already aiming for an annual economic growth rate of 6 per cent. More competititve export prices and cheaper tourism may improve the economy and attract investment in Senegal, but things will be unstable for a long time to come. Much of the country's production depends on imports of fuel and agro-chemicals, and profit margins for producers were already very tight before devaluation. The government's 'Buy Local' campaign should help, but old habits die hard, particularly in a country where devaluation is a totally new experience. The government also hopes to restrict consumer demand and keep inflation below that of its neighbours. It has had some limited success in terms of reducing budget deficits, but the improvement has been bought at high social cost: health and welfare services have been cut, and rural producers left high and dry without the subsidies and technical support which they used to depend on.

Without proper health care or education, it is the children of the poor who bear the brunt of the government's 'structural adjustment' policies

Away from it all

Could tourism become a major source of national income? Senegal has palm-fringed tropical beaches and luxury hotels, exotic music, and colourful markets. Tours across the fascinating Sahelian landscape and canoe trips through the lush greenery of mangrove swamps are some of the attractions that bring visitors to Senegal.

By the late 1980s, tourism was already the country's third biggest foreign-exchange earner, earning enough to pay for much of its petroleum and rice imports. But the experience of many other developing countries has shown that betting on tourism as a means to generate resources for development can be a dangerous game.

Most of the investment in tourist facilities by the government and foreign leisure companies has gone into building luxury hotels and beach complexes. While producing revenue for the government, many of these make little contribution to the local economy, since they import most of their furniture and equipment from Europe, and even a lot of the food for their guests. Besides, the foreign companies take home their profits, with the net result that 60 per cent of the economic benefit of Senegal's tourist business is lost to the country.

Another risk for the government is that big investments could turn sour and leave them with more debt if European holiday-makers, who are the most numerous, decide to go elsewhere. Recently, for example, violence in the Casamance region brought tourism there to a halt.

More hopefully, there have been some efforts to develop an 'alternative tourism' for people keen to experience the real life of Senegal. Simple camps with thatched huts have been built by village people, using local materials and techniques, which enable visitors to participate in some aspects of ordinary life. In this way the local community gets the economic benefits of providing accommodation, meals, and other services, and the surplus can be used to improve their living conditions.

Tourism brings alien cultural influences to the streets of Dakar

When aid is not the answer

WHATEVER THE SETBACKS elsewhere, in one economic arena Senegal has been outstandingly successful — namely, in attracting overseas aid. From $240 million in 1980, income from foreign assistance soared to $740 million in 1990, representing on paper $100 for every man, woman, and child in the country — four times more than the average for West Africa. President Diouf has established a solid reputation in the world of international diplomacy, and he knows how to play his cards. With the end of the Cold War, Senegal — like many other African countries — lost its strategic importance for the superpowers, who no longer needed to prop up friendly regimes for ideological reasons. With an eye to staying in credit with Washington, Senegal sent a contingent of troops to support the allied forces in the Gulf War. It was a good bet, especially as next-door Mauritania was seen to be backing Saddam Hussein. More recently, despite the goodwill which this gesture earned, aid commitments are beginning to decline, though perhaps less than they might have done otherwise.

During the 1980s it was another story. Prompted by the plight of a drought-stricken Sahel, Northern governments and UN agencies poured in a stream of project money. There were other reasons, too. As aid donors belatedly began to bang the drum for democratisation in Africa, Senegal was the shining example they wanted everyone to emulate. To support democracy in Senegal, the US aid programme pumped in dollars; the flow reached a peak of $62 million in 1986 and is still over $40 million a year. For comparison, the British government's bilateral assistance to Senegal is just over $1 million, although it contributes significantly more through the European Union's aid programme. But where does all the foreign assistance go? It tends to be spent on big capital-intensive projects which are not relevant to the needs of small communities, like the phosphate plant near Thiès, pictured below.

Phosphate plant near Thiès: with aid from the European Union and World Bank, Senegal plans to spend US$110m on developing its phosphate industry; but demand on the world market is falling, and the mines may prove to be white elephants

JEREMY HARTLEY/OXFAM

By the people, for the people

Real development in the village of Dimar

Ten years ago, the women of the village of Dimar, on the Senegal River, had little contact with the outside world. Apart from all their tiring household duties, they had no productive work except to labour in their husbands' fields. That was the way things had always been, and they had little chance of changing it on their own.

Then some people from an independent development group in Thiès arrived and started asking questions. They encouraged the women to form their own village group and helped them to start a vegetable-growing project. It was the first time the women of Dimar had ever got together to do something for themselves independently of their menfolk, and — to begin with — the men didn't like it. But the project went well, the women began to earn money from selling their carrots, onions, cabbages, and tomatoes, and soon other villages joined in.

Today, the development group, Maisons Familiales Rurales, has 1,200 members in 11 villages around Dimar — and one-third of them are men, who have begun to realise that working together is good for them as well. All the local villages hold their markets on different days of the week, so the women can go around from one to the other, selling their vegetables. With the profits, and some

> 'It's not just the money that we get from the group. It's sharing problems and ideas. Before, we were each alone. Now we are all one person.' — *A member of the PROFEMU women's group, Thiès*

JEREMY HARTLEY/OXFAM

Dimar Dieri village, near Ndioum: a cereal bank managed by the villagers themselves, and supported by Maisons Familiales Rurales. It buys up locally grown grain, stores it, and sells it to people later in the year at prices they can afford.

help from MFR, each village has now established a cereal bank. Five storage units have been built at Dimar for the cereal bank pro-gramme, and the community contributed about £600 (six per cent of the cost). As a result they have been able to buy 65,000 tons of paddy rice and 3,000 tons of sorghum. Without a storage place, they previously had to sell all their crops and hope to be able to buy back enough for their needs — often at inflated prices — at the end of the dry season.

This is real development: the kind that changes people's lives measurably for the better.

A vacuum to fill

Maisons Familiales Rurales is one of hundreds of voluntary organisations operating in Senegal, working directly with poor communities, and largely run

> 'Our husbands used to complain about us coming home late from work, but now we're bringing in money, they say, "Haven't you got another meeting to go to?"' — *A member of the PROFEMU women's group in Pikine, Dakar*

by Senegalese people themselves. MFR has 55 local associations; one of their main objectives is to encourage village people to stay in the countryside and not join the exodus to the towns. Its members are farmers, pastoralists, fishing people, and artisans. They get training in how to improve production techniques, protect natural resources, improve health and hygiene, acquire literacy, and run savings and credit schemes.

Some of the grassroots associations work in a small way on a local level, like the Rural Development Union which works with village women near the town of Thiès on a range of projects, from growing henna and selling smoked fish to breeding goats and organising literacy classes. Others are much larger, and one — a federation of village groups called FONGS — represents over one million small farmers all over Senegal.

Acronyms abound in this area. There is ENDA (Environment and Development Action), which undertakes research and grassroots development in areas ranging from health, renewable energy, and unemployment, to debt and structural adjustment. ... There is RADI (African Network for Integrated Development), which provides services to farmers along the Senegal River, supplying seeds, running a repair workshop for farm machinery, and offering help with marketing. ... And there is PROFEMU (Programme des Femmes en Milieu Urbain), which supports women's groups in poor neighbourhoods of Dakar and Thiès, providing start-up capital for all kinds of small enterprises, advice on legal rights, and family-planning services.

'It has changed the way men see us'

In the remote Ferlo region of north-east Senegal, the Fulani people depend on rearing livestock for much of their income. But long spells of drought have shrivelled up much of the grazing land. Undernourished animals are prone to disease, and expert help is far away.

Now ADENA, a local association of community groups, is training selected villagers in the prevention of disease. Many of the trainees are women. In the words of Maimouna Mamoudou Lam Ba: 'Women are often left alone here when the men go away to find work. I used to lose many animals to diseases, but now I know how to treat them. It has changed the way men see us. At first, the men shied away from accepting advice on the care of their animals from women. Now the women have shown there is nothing the men can do that women can't do also!'

Namarel village, Ferlo region: a literacy class run by ADENA, a local development association

The associations vary in size and experience, but the best of them have one thing in common: they are helping to fill the vacuum left after the government's withdrawal from the supply of social services, and to cushion the shock of structural adjustment policies in poor communities.

New directions for women

Some of the most dynamic of the voluntary associations work with women, bringing them together to find ways to enlarge the scope of their lives. Under religious and secular law, women's status in Senegal is inferior to that of men; girls have fewer educational opportunities, are often married off at an early age, and are usually kept in ignorance of their economic and human rights. But support groups all over Senegal are now helping women with education and literacy, and credit or technical assistance with their own businesses, as well as health care and information on their legal rights.

Madame Binta Sarr, president of the Senegalese Association for the Advancement of Women (APROFES), says: 'What has changed most for women in the villages is the progress they've made towards taking charge of their own lives. Now they are able to plan things for themselves, and some women leaders are emerging from within the communities.'

No easy answers

There are no easy answers to the economic and social problems that beset Senegal. But the 'associative movement', with its committed leadership, and its closeness to poor communities, is certainly an important force for development. Many foreign voluntary organisations are shifting the weight of their programmes from one-off projects to longer-term support for organisations within the movement — which is just as well, because it can no longer rely on help from the government in Dakar.

Cash-cropping: a vicious circle

JEREMY HARTLEY/OXFAM

Hard choices for Ndam Mor Fademba: vegetables are thirsty plants, and water is scarce; millet won't grow in the weed-ridden soil; peanuts will grow (for a time), but they don't pay — and they need fertiliser; fertiliser costs too much. More and more young people are leaving the village.

A visit to a village

The village of Ndam Mor Fademba? 'Yes, it's over there, a few kilometres,' says the man in the Mickey Mouse t-shirt, standing beside his hut and gesturing across the dusty Sahelian landscape. There are scrubby thorn trees, but no sign of a road or track. 'I'll accompany you,' he adds with a smile, and climbs aboard the vehicle.

Ndam Mor Fademba is a community of about 600 people in the Kayar region of northern Senegal. As in thousands of other villages scattered across the country, its people grow cereals, peanuts and vegetables, and keep some animals; but their land has suffered severely from 20 years of recurrent drought and the pressure of human activities.

Founded 200 years ago, Ndam Mor Fademba was first settled by a family of *marabouts*, whose descendants are still dominant in village life. In the central square there is a mosque and a school, both with lighting from a solar panel provided by a US agency, as well as the family compounds of the village leaders. The village also has its own cemetery, a football field, and a peanut co-operative.

Near the blackboard in the schoolroom is a pile of exercise books containing the pupils' neatly-written dictations in French. One, on the subject of 'Our Village', notes that 'The big square has a large silk-cotton tree, where people meet in its shade.' The teacher admits there is a little historical licence here: sadly, the silk-cotton tree died some time ago.

Many species of tree — some of them valuable for food, medicines, or construction timber — have disappeared from the area as the climate has become more arid, or as a result of land clearance for peanuts. But there has been some replanting in the village itself, making it an oasis of shade and greenery in an otherwise dried-up landscape.

Using water from a tube well, women cultivate potatoes, onions, aubergines, and cabbages. But when the motor pump lifting water from the well broke down some time ago, the American agency replaced it with a windmill, which the villagers complain gives a very inadequate flow. There are also three hand-dug wells, used mainly for watering livestock; but shortage of water, they say, is their biggest continuing problem.

Since the onset of the drought, most families, who previously relied entirely on crops, have taken to keeping some animals as well. Though they are almost all Wolof agriculturalists, they can no longer live from their crops. As one poorer farmer put it, 'In years of good rainfall, our harvest used to produce eight or nine months of food, or in average years at least five to six months' supply. But in the bad years like those at present, the harvest lasts only two or three months.'

For all their worries, the people of Ndam Mor Fademba are better off than many other rural communities, perhaps because of their maraboutic connections. In particular, the children have the chance to learn French, Wolof, or (at a Koranic school in one of the nearby villages) Arabic. The village has its own oil press and a mill for grinding millet into flour, donated by a foreign agency.

But the problem which haunts the farmers of Ndam is the sharply declining fertility of their soils. It has brought an invasion of the parasitic weed *striga*, which can devastate millet crops and has forced them to switch to growing peanuts.

Water is a precious commodity for villages like Ndam Mor Fademba

JEREMY HARTLEY/OXFAM

See Naples, Ndiaye

The village association of Ndam Mor Fademba now has at least one outpost in Italy, which has become a favourite destination for the village's young migrant workers. Some go to other European countries or to Dakar, so that the active people left in the village are mostly women and older men.

Money sent home by the migrant workers makes a vital contribution to family income. In addition, the group in Italy meets at least once a year to send a collective contribution for the annual religious festival. It also offers a 'welcome service' to new arrivals from the village, covering all their subsistence costs for three months until they get settled and find work.

Housewives' choice

Unlike the farmers of Ndam Mor Fademba, peasants in other parts of Senegal are reducing their peanut fields and planting more of the traditional food crops: millet and sorghum. The reason is simple: they can't earn enough from the sale of peanuts to buy the food they need for themselves, so it's safer just to grow their own.

This, of course, has the effect of reducing exports, so the government has less foreign exchange with which to import food for the urban population or to help farmers increase their productivity. It is a vicious circle with no obvious way out. According to one authority, peasant peanut producers earned more for their daily labour in 1913 than in 1984, and things have got worse, if anything, since then. But with more than a million people dependent on it, there is no way the government can abandon the peanut economy; they will simply have to keep propping it up with costly price subsidies, just to prevent a total collapse.

Even with the subsidies, it is not economic for farmers to use the quantity of chemical fertiliser that would be necessary to protect the soil, nor to leave land fallow to restore itself. So large areas of arable land are being 'mined' of their nutrients until they can no longer sustain a crop, and then abandoned. According to the UN's Food and Agriculture Organisation, if soil degradation in the Sahel is not controlled, the region will soon be able to feed only half the number of people which it used to be able to support.

The government's declared aim of reaching 80 per cent food self-sufficiency by the year 2000 would require the rural population to produce almost twice its own needs, in order to feed the towns. In fact, current production trends are almost all going in the wrong direction — and an official campaign which has been trying for several years to persuade urban consumers back to traditional cereals, in order to reduce imports of wheat and rice, has almost admitted defeat.

Rice and wheatflour are the city's convenience foods. Housewives tend to reject millet and sorghum, because they take too long to prepare and cook. Even in small provincial towns, the French baguette from a local bakery — as crisp and fresh as any in Paris — has become a symbol of modern living. Some may be made from food-aid wheat, but an increasing share of imports has to be paid for.

Macoumba Diop and his son raking over last year's millet stubble; this year they plan to try peanuts. But the soil's nutrients are exhausted, and, without government subsidies, they can't afford fertiliser.

Rice at a price

WITHIN LIVING MEMORY, the Senegal River Valley was a very different place from today. The river was the main route for transport and travel; wildlife, including lions and hippopotami, abounded. Farmers grew millet on sandy upland fields, away from the river, and sorghum on the valley floor when it flooded after the rainy season. Farther away from the river, the dry Ferlo region was home to semi-nomadic pastoral communities, with their large herds of cattle, sheep, and goats. But now there is a tarmac road all the way from St Louis to Bakel. Much of the rich land of the flood plain is under threat. Most of the wildlife has gone. And irrigated rice fields, spreading along the river banks, bar the way to the herders' livestock, which used to be watered there in the dry season.

In recent decades the government has been developing irrigated rice schemes, managed by its parastatal agencies. But far more dramatic changes were promised with the building of two large dams to harness the river waters. In 1975 the three main countries on the banks of the river — Senegal, Mauritania, and Mali — formed the Senegal Valley Development Authority (OMVS) to finance, build, and manage the dams, By the time they were formally declared open in 1992, the massive Manantali dam in Mali and the smaller Diama dam near St Louis had cost close to $1 billion — a monumentally misjudged investment which is unlikely to achieve any of its proclaimed objectives in the foreseeable future, and has cost the country a large slice of its foreign debt.

Manantali, it was promised, would produce enough hydro-electricity to keep Dakar lit up for 100 years. It would make the river navigable as far as Kayes, in Mali, giving the Sahelian interior an important outlet to the sea; and it would permit irrigated farming on 350,000 hectares of land, two-thirds of it in Senegal.

Diama dam across the River Senegal between Mauritania and Senegal: one reason for Senegal's external debt, which totalled US$3.7 billion in 1991 (the latest available figure)

A pump to irrigate rice fields along the River Senegal near Mbagam village. Irrigation used to be subsidised but now, under the government's structural adjustment programme, local farmers have to pay the full cost.

and smaller plates in front. There are two large beds, stools for seating, a collection of framed photographs on the walls, and an embroidered panel of Mecca.

The discussion turns to cattle-raising in other countries, and the intensive systems of European farms, where animals are fattened in sheds under controlled conditions and rarely graze on pasture. One of the villagers, recently trained as an auxiliary vet, nods thoughtfully. 'That's the direction we need to go as well.' His face betrays the sadness of someone pronouncing the epitaph for a whole way of life.

But his words also contain hope: a readiness to consider change and even to look for it. The village president agrees with him, though he says that theirs is still the view of a minority. The first need is to find forage crops that can thrive in this arid climate. Unfortunately, a first experiment with some plants that do well in the Australian outback has not been successful, but they will keep on trying.

Self-help in action

Peulh pastoralists do not sit around waiting for outsiders to solve their problems for them. Some young men from the village of Namarel, studying in Dakar, got together in 1989 to form a development association for Namarel, Yoly, and the surrounding villages. They called a village meeting at which five problems were singled out for attention: health, literacy, women's development, water supply, and animal health.

They called their association ADENA, and within three years it had 3,000 members. It began with a network of 37 veterinary auxiliaries and a literacy programme. The latest plans include a community health programme, a network of forestry volunteers to protect the natural environment, a revolving fund for cattle marketing, the purchase of a grinding mill for village women, and a theatre group to stimulate debate on community issues through song, dance, and drama.

Facing page: Yoly village: in the house of Chief Oumar Ba (seated right)

Namarel village: arithmetic class organised by ADENA

Pastoralists in
Senegal face a
doubtful future

JEREMY HARTLEY/OXFAM

Pastoralism under siege

Pastoral communities are besieged from
many sides. The crisis they face today has
been gathering for 100 years and is
impelled by many forces, notably the
growth of towns and the expansion of
agriculture, which have forced herding
communities back into the most arid and
marginal zones. The process continues, and
— apart from their daily struggle to protect
themselves against an increasingly erratic
climate and the threat of famine — they are
under pressure from farmers, who are
appropriating more and more of their
traditional grazing lands for agriculture.

Pressure also comes from the
government in Dakar. In 1991 a Presidential decree handed over to the
powerful Mouride brotherhood 45,000
hectares of what was supposed to be a
protected forest in the centre of the
country. Six thousand herders and 100,000
animals grazing there were forced off the
land. In a matter of weeks, the forest of
Khelkom had been flattened by teams of
the Mouride faithful from all over the
country. Five million trees and bushes
were uprooted in what was one of the last
remaining forests of Senegal's degraded
heartland. Some foreign donors, officially

committed to helping to protect the
country's environment, and whose
objections might have had some effect,
chose instead to turn a blind eye.

On the first anniversary of this event, a
national 'Khelkom Support Committee'
issued a statement asserting that the
forest's destruction was not an isolated
phenomenon, but 'the result of policies of
the Senegalese government which often
lead to violent confrontations between
farmers and pastoralists'. The government
made no reply.

In one rural community over a ten-year
period, the Mourides put in six per cent of
the applications for land grants, but they
received 62 per cent of the land allotted,
much of it classified for grazing or forest.
Herders are on a hiding to nothing when
it comes to seeking land rights. Applicants
have to show that the land will be put to
'productive use' — and, by the official
definition, pasture is simply not consid-
ered productive.

The Khelkom peanut fields may
produce an annual crop worth $2 million
— for a few years. After that, the soil is
exhausted and blown away, and likely to
be reduced to desert.

Facing page:
Inoculating cattle in
Loumbol village,
Ferlo region

34

The harvest of the sea

ON THE SAND DUNES of the Tongue of Barbary, a thin strip of land extending across the mouth of the Senegal River, the fishermen of St Louis long ago made their cemetery. Looking out over the sea where many men have met their fate, the simple graves are draped with fishing nets and other seafarers' mementoes.

These days, for the mourning families who come here, grief is often mingled with anger. As competition for a declining catch gets fiercer, local in-shore fishermen are being killed along the coast of Senegal at the rate of almost one a week, their *pirogues* — large canoes — smashed in collisions with industrial boats poaching at night inside the prohibited six-mile zone. Occasionally the captains of intruding boats are taken to court, but they have political influence and good lawyers, and they are seldom punished. If the crew of the *pirogue* survive such a collision, they are probably out of business: a new boat would cost them about £2,000..

Big fish, big business

Senegal's 33,000 independent fishermen have many hazards to face. Although they account for about three-quarters of the annual catch and 40 per cent of fish exports, they get no say in Senegal's agreements with the European Union. The 1991/92 agreement gave 86 European vessels the right to fish in Senegalese waters, for which they paid about £15 million a year. For 1993/94, a new agreement extended the EU's fishing rights — including a 59 per cent increase in the quota for deep-water species — while their payment to the government of Senegal was raised by 11 per cent. In the

long run, fishing stocks will be exhausted, but in the short term the government in Dakar needs the revenue, so the authorities are not keen to rock the boat when it comes to a few accidents or a bit of poaching.

The agreements stipulate that European vessels should have an observer on board, respect quotas, and sell a portion of their catch in Senegal. But, according to the small fishermen, these terms are not enforced and there is no control on their dumping of the unwanted, lower-quality fish they catch. Some estimate that the industrial boats dump back in the sea as much as 40 per cent of their catch.

To campaign for fairer treatment and better conditions, the artisanal fishermen have formed themselves into West Africa's first fishermen's union, the CNPS. The union is demanding that the in-shore zone reserved for them be extended from six to 12 miles. CNPS wants the European boats to be equipped to detect *pirogues* in the dark, and to be clearly identified, so they can be traced if they infringe the rules. Otherwise there's no chance of catching them: Senegal has only one coastguard vessel and one aircraft to police 700 km of coastline.

Declining fish stocks are affecting fishing communities and consumers alike. High-value fish once commonly eaten in Senegal are now routinely exported, or bought only by the elite in Dakar. And all the time, cheaper fish are becoming less abundant.

At the old Lébou fishing village of Yoff, outside Dakar, a prominent buyer on the beach recently was an Egyptian businessman, accompanied by a team of workers packing newly-landed fish into ice-boxes for shipment to the USA. Once mainly a

local industry, fishing has become big international business. In St Louis, competition comes not only from the Europeans, but also from Korean pick-up boats. These vessels can take on board as many as 40 *pirogues* and their crews. They transport them to well-stocked waters farther down the African coast — sometimes as far as Gabon — and there act as mother ship for a month or more, while the *pirogues* do their fishing for them.

The CNPS union alleges that conditions for the fishermen on these boats are inhuman, with water and food rationed. But Maguatte Sangharé, the head of a family fishing cooperative in St Louis which has worked on the pick-up boats, has no such complaints. Without them, he says, a lot of fishermen would have no hope, whereas they can come back from a six-week trip with 3-4 tons of fish per *pirogue*. They are paid 175 francs a kilo for 'European' fish such as sea bream and 125 francs for 'African' species, which are sold locally. Since they live on the boats, the fishermen have few costs. Eight pick-up boats now provide work for about 200 *pirogues*. The Korean boats are actually based at Las Palmas in the Canary Islands.

Even without intruding trawlers, the *pirogue* crews working from the shore are often dicing with death when they set out. For two or three months a year the Atlantic rollers are so violent that crossing the bar becomes virtually impossible. Even under better conditions the *pirogues* toss alarmingly as they plough through the breakers, and from the safety of the beach the helmsman standing at the stern in his oilskins can be seen lurching up and down like a tiny yellow yo-yo.

Spécialités de la maison

The art of the kitchen has a place of honour in Senegalese life. The original national cuisine is flavoured by a taste of Arabic, French, and other African dishes.

Tiep-bou-dien (fish-with-rice) is the centre-piece of Senegalese cooking, making best use of the Atlantic catch, which includes sea bass, tuna, mullet, Nile perch, swordfish, and many kinds of shellfish. The fish is cooked in oil and onion, accompanied by cabbage, carrots, tomato sauce, and rice, prepared in the fish and vegetable stock.

Other favourite dishes are *yassa*, which can be chicken, lamb, or fish marinated in lemon juice, red pepper, and onion and then charcoal-grilled; *maffé*, a sort of chicken or lamb stew with vegetables and peanut paste; and the national variety of couscous, made with millet and flavoured with baobab leaves.

The biggest feast of the year is *Tabaski*, the Muslim Feast of the Lamb, when every family sacrifices a sheep as a sign of faith, symbolically following God's instruction to Abraham to sacrifice his son. For this occasion, some 200,000 sheep are slaughtered each year and many families have to save throughout the year to buy one. Traditionally, they are killed by a member of the family, but many of the younger generation are losing the skill, and professional slaughterers can be called in. The skins of the animals are then stretched out on the ground, covered with ash. After three days they are dry and are then used as prayer mats.

Apart from meat, fish, and its staple cereals, Senegal has an abundance of tropical fruits. The mango season is eagerly awaited each year, while guava, tamarind, coconut, and pineapple are all used to make fruit juices or conserves.

Family meals are most often completed with tea: a green China tea with fresh mint. Elaborately prepared, the tea is brewed three times and served in small glasses, the first strong, the third milder and sweeter.

Pounding millet for the evening meal, Mewell village

less and less politically feasible as the population balance swings to the cities.

With 1.5 million people, the Greater Dakar region now has 20 per cent of the country's population, crammed into less than one per cent of its territory. The capital alone has four-fifths of the nation's businesses, three-quarters of all permanent jobs, and three-quarters of all vehicles. Most of the food eaten by the town-dwellers has to be imported, and the peasants unwittingly help to pay for that, in terms of reduced investment and services.

If Dakar absorbs much more than its share of national resources, one thing that must be said is that it has an effective government. Mayor Mamadou Diop, elected for the first time in 1984, has won popularity with some major investments to improve schools and health services, as well as up-grading the city's markets, public gardens, and playing fields. With Dakar still growing at a dizzy rate, he has a lot to do.

High fashion in hairstyles, displayed in a Dakar market

JEREMY HARTLEY/OXFAM

Putting on the style

Whatever the problems of urban growth, there is no denying the spirit and vitality of Dakar, which stands at the crossroads of African and European cultures, with its fine buildings, the hubbub of busy markets, and its almost perfect climate. Down the wide, tree-lined avenues of the old colonial centre, past cafés and smart shops, stroll wealthy Dakarois, sleek and poised in their traditional dress: the epitome of West African elegance.

Clothes and grooming have always been important to the better-off Senegalese families. Hairstyles, in particular, used to be very elaborate. Each family had its own style, so that it constituted a form of personal identity. Up to adolescence, boys as well as girls had their specific styles, but at that age the boys shaved their heads completely. A girl adopted a different hairstyle when she married, including a braid up to the crown of her head, as a sign of eternal union with her husband.

Sometimes, new styles were created to mark important events: candidates in an election would even have 'campaign hairdos' invented for their supporters to wear. But although a few survive, many of the traditional forms of hairdressing have disappeared since today's grandmothers were young. Some styles took days to complete and were difficult to maintain. Now, people have less time, and simpler styles have become the fashion, in clothes as in coiffure. There is, nevertheless, a strong and perhaps growing interest in forms of cultural expression that assert the national identity — and nothing has diminished the aesthetic sense of the Senegalese and their appreciation of elegance.

Night-time in the shanty-town

ONLY A STONE'S THROW away from the bright lights of central Dakar is a *bidonville*: a ramshackle shanty town consisting of long rows of corrugated tin huts. Here live the forgotten people, the poorest of the urban poor.

In a little open space, a stately silk-cotton tree spreads its massive roots. In the maze of alleyways that surround it there are mounds of car parts and old iron waiting to be recycled, a vegetable garden tended by the women of this tin town, and one or two tiny kiosks selling basic supplies like soap and matches. Groups of men sit round glowing braziers in the darkness, talking, smoking. Others pass by like ghosts, exchanging polite greetings.

The shacks are mostly one-room homes, some papered with pages from magazines, others bare. There is just room for one or two beds and some floor space for sleeping mats. No windows. But people have their pride. The shacks are kept as clean as conditions allow, and the residents are getting on with their lives as best they can. The pregnancy rate is high, but there is relatively little prostitution within the community, and little or no violence. Theft, of course, is something else. Pointing to his van, one man grimaces: 'I have to sleep in it, if I don't want it stripped.'

Despite the overcrowding and the lack of the most basic services, there's no time for despondency for people who want to eat tomorrow. In fact, the *bidonvilles* of Dakar have quite a developed economy of their own. The men are mechanics, petty traders, or experts in repairs and recycling. The women take in washing from the neighbourhood, run little cafés in the alleyways, or work on the vegetable plot. One woman won £500 in a lottery a few years ago and invested in a large refrigerator. With it she makes ice to sell, and she rents space to people who want to keep food or drinks cold. She hopes that one of her eight children will get an education in order to support the family later.

For such people, education is the shining hope of economic liberation. A family of 10 all live in one room, with no furniture except the beds; but the five school-age girls persevere with their homework, proud of their exercise books and instruction sheets for a basic literacy course in French. Hardly any of the shanty-town children go to school, but the local voluntary organisation, ENDA, is helping with the literacy training. ENDA is also supporting a young man who gives free evening classes in French, English, and Arabic. He has a blackboard installed at the roadside.

But for those who have nothing, there is still no security. This *bidonville* is owned by a foreign company which now wants to evict the whole community and sell the land for development.

JEREMY HARTLEY/OXFAM

A seamstress at work in a shanty-town on the edge of Dakar

The family first

FAMILY TIES come before anything else in most of Africa, and in Senegal that is certainly the case. The extended family is not just a question of having lots of aunts and uncles and cousins: the bonds of the family are much stronger than that. Among the Wolof, each member of the family has a clearly defined role and responsibilities in relation to everyone else, and their lives are woven together in a complex fabric which can resist many kinds of stress.

The Wolof view of the cosmos relates every person to his or her ancestors, the family line, and the spirit world. It is bound up with a theory of reincarnation, and a new baby is therefore a manifestation of the spirit of the ancestors, a tangible link between past, present, and future. The child is brought up with a consciousness of its place in this family pantheon. In due course he or she acquires another lifetime bond, this time outside the family: a bond with all those of the same age group in the community. Taken together, these relationships build a world-view in which individuals see themselves first and foremost as part of a spiritual and temporal collective. Some aspects of this world-view may be particular to the Wolof, but it is generally shared by the other ethnic groups of Senegal, for whom the self-centred individualism of Western societies is very far removed.

This, at least in principle, is how it should be. In practice, faced with new economic and social pressures, many

Merina Diop village, near Pekesse: Anta Mbaya, traditional birth attendant (left), advises a mother about the care of her new baby

BERNARD TAYLOR/OXFAM

44

families in the towns and cities cannot give their children this traditional education within the family circle. When both parents have to work, children in poorer neighbourhoods are often left unsupervised, with no one to explain the world around them. Among the urban bourgeoisie, meanwhile, traditional values are giving way to the more material concerns of the nuclear family, which leaves the business of educating the children to formal schools.

A question of numbers

Polygamy was permitted by the traditional religions of Senegal, so the country's conversion to Islam, rather than Christianity, posed no problems in this regard. In the old days, in an underpopulated country where all families worked on the land, it made economic sense for a man to have 15 to 20 children to join the family workforce, and he probably needed three or four wives to achieve that. At the present time, about one quarter of married men have more than one wife, but the number is declining as lifestyles change. Younger people in the cities are almost unanimous in rejecting polygamy. This may help to slow the nation's birthrate, bearing in mind that wives in polygamous families often compete to have the most children.

Another factor in this trend is women's progress towards emancipation, which is giving many a new sense of independence, and the confidence to develop their own talents. Sonja Fagerberg Diallo, a leading literacy campaigner, says there has been a tremendous social change among women who have learned to read and write, creating a wide gap between the under-40 age group and their mothers. But the impact of this change, she adds, has yet to come. Senegalese society equates wisdom with age, so for the time being the younger women defer, saying, 'It's not our turn yet.'

Most girls marry at 16 or 17 and have their first baby before they are 20. On average they will have about six children, though girls who have been to school place less value on large families than those without an education.

The mortality rates for children remain higher than in other regions of Africa: 18 children in every 100 die before the age of five (compared with 13 in Southern Africa), the main causes being malaria, diarrhoea, respiratory infections and measles — often made lethal by underlying malnutrition. Nearly one-third of children do not get an adequate diet.

Senegal's population rose from an estimated one million at the turn of the century to about 2.5 million in the 1950s, and to 7.5 million in 1990. Some of this growth has been due to inward migration

Traditionally children learn about the world at their mother's knee

BERNARD TAYLOR/OXFAM

from the Sahara and countries to the south, but primarily to a dramatic decline in the mortality rate. In the past, mortality in the Sahel was roughly equal to the birthrate, and thus an equilibrium was maintained. But since the early years of this century it has dropped by more than half, largely because of extensive vaccination campaigns and other forms of preventative medicine.

The people of Senegal will have to cope somehow with their rapid growth in numbers, but family-planning campaigns, despite having lots of American aid money behind them, have encountered stiff resistance. The age-old attachment to large families is still strong, backed by the pro-natalist attitudes of Islam, Catholicism, and the traditional religions. For the poor, anyhow, limiting births is not an intelligent strategy; the more children you have, the better your chances that one of them will do well and be able to support the family.

What's in a name?

For *Smith, Brown, Jenkins,* and *McNeil,* read *Ndiaye, Sow, Thiam, Cissokho,* and *Diedhiou.* With the British names, you can guess whether their owners are from England, Scotland, or Wales; but if a Smith meets a Smith, they are unlikely to assume that they are related to each other. It is different in Senegal. If a Ndiaye (pronounced *N'j-eye*) meets another Ndiaye, they know that they must be cousins. Names here are important and, along with distinctive features, modes of dress, and manners, are a badge of one's ethnic origins. This counts for something in a country with as many as 20 distinct ethnic groups. Four-fifths of the population, however, is made up of five groups: Wolof (40 per cent), Serer (14 per cent), Peulh (12 per cent), Toucouleur (10.5 per cent), and Diola (5.3 per cent).

The Senegalese sense of humour finds particular expression in the many 'teasing relationships' that exist between families and sometimes between ethnic groups. With a grin, a Serer may remind a Toucouleur that he would have been his slave once upon a time. When a Gueye meets a Seck, one of them is almost bound to make a joke about the other's inordinate appetite for rice.

While each ethnic group remains attached to its own traditions, the dominance of the Wolof is reflected in the widespread adoption of their language throughout the country. This process of 'wolofisation' means that 80 per cent of people now speak this tongue, while about a quarter speak the Peulh language, Pulaar. All the same, French remains the official language, even though it is spoken only by a small educated minority.

Schools without books, clinics without medicines

A PRIMARY SCHOOL TEACHER in Kaolack is trying to explain why only one Senegalese child in seven passes the exams at the end of primary school. 'They have to share books. Quite often there are no notebooks or pens. Sometimes there isn't even a school building, and the parents have to contribute to build one. The situation is disastrous.'

Fewer than two-thirds of children in Senegal go to primary school, and it's not because they're playing truant: there just aren't the places. This rate of enrolment compares with the 95 per cent achieved by other African countries at the same level of development. Forced to make budget cuts in order to meet its targets for economic structural adjustment, the government's approach has been to keep all the teachers on the payroll, but to stop investing in school buildings, and in essential equipment.

More than half of those who fail the primary exam abandon their studies; a third will try again; and 10 per cent will go to private schools. By 1988, because of the breakdown of state education, private schools accounted for almost 20 per cent of secondary pupils.

Only two per cent of the nation's students attend university. But in 1988/89, a quarter of the education budget went to higher education. It just happens that the undergraduates and their professors have important political clout. All the same, the reputation of the University of Dakar has suffered from a doubling of student numbers in five years and a decline in teaching standards, which has led to a high drop-out rate in many faculties. Strikes by teachers and students are common. At the impressive new

> 'There are no schools in our village. The nearest is 9 km away, with no means of getting there. That's the government for you. School is free, but for a good education you have to pay. It's a 9 km walk to the health centre, too — and you have to pay for everything when you get there.'
> — *A villager from Sare Souky*

University of St Louis, the students went on strike in 1993 over the shortage of teaching staff and the government's failure to release their grants.

0.8 of a dentist

The situation is not much different in the health sector, which has been the hardest hit by government austerity measures. For every 100,000 people, there are six doctors, three pharmacists, and exactly 0.8 of a dentist. Nearly half of all health workers are concentrated in Dakar. Four out of five people in the cities have access to clean water, but in the rural areas. the figure is more like one in four.

Dimar village: a roof but no desks in the primary school

BERNARD TAYLOR/OXFAM

Dimar village: bandages but no medicines in the health clinic

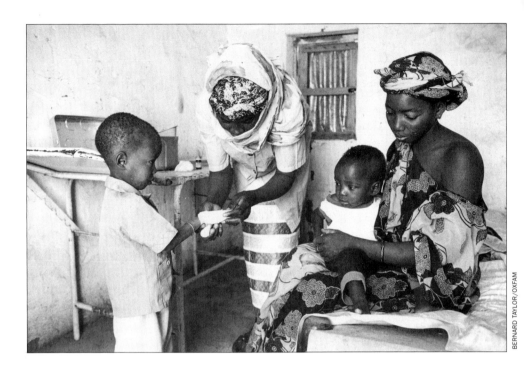

Under the structural adjustment reforms, people now have to pay for a visit to the doctor and for any medicines they need. These charges are based on the principle of cost recovery, which the World Bank says is 'perfectly accepted by the users of public health services'. Perhaps the principle is accepted, but in practice by the late 1980s fewer people were going to a doctor or to hospital than 10 years earlier — and few would claim that was because they were healthier.

By 1990, salaries were devouring three-quarters of the health budget. There was only five per cent left for medicines, and the lion's share of that went to hospitals, leaving little or nothing to fill the empty shelves of village health centres. Although professional salaries may be very high compared with other West African countries, it would be hard to argue that Senegal's health services are over-staffed.

Perhaps it would be more efficient to reduce the numbers of health workers in order to buy more medicines and equipment; but would they serve more, or fewer, patients? These are not Alice-in-Wonderland questions; on the contrary, they are typical of the harsh choices that confront Senegal's decision makers every day.

Statistics don't tell the whole truth

At the level of statistical analysis, the prospects for an upturn in the provision of schooling and health care are not encouraging. But, as in many areas of Senegalese life, the people's perception of their reality transcends the gloom of statisticians. Schools, for example, are not the only repositories of knowledge for children, and many young Senegalese have learned about the modern world from being actively involved in their own rapidly changing environment. This kind of knowledge is not measured by formal education, but it may nevertheless be a good preparation for life in the world they will inherit.

Rumblings of discontent

THROUGH LONG YEARS of drought and economic decline, the Senegalese have tolerated increasing hardship without any sign of revolt against the system. But they will rebel violently against what they see as blatant injustice. After the 1988 Presidential elections, when the opposition parties claimed they were cheated by vote-rigging, protests went on for several months.

The Casamance in revolt

For the past ten years, a sense of injustice has also fanned the flames of a separatist movement among the Diola people of the Casamance. Almost cut off physically from the rest of Senegal by the intervening territory of the Gambia, the Diola have preserved much of their traditional way of life from outside influences. They have always resented the intrusion of northerners in their affairs, and consider they've had a raw deal from central government. A steady influx of peasants, fishermen, and proselytising Muslims — along with foreign tourists at a Club Méditerranée resort and other beach hotels — is seen as a new colonial invasion. Land has been allocated to influential families from the north and some of the Diolas' sacred groves have been felled to plant peanut fields.

The Diola have never taken kindly to foreign domination. A French Governor-General in 1917 admitted, 'We are not the masters of the Casamance; we are only tolerated there.' One problem for outsiders trying to assert their authority here is that Diola society has no castes or hierarchies, only an assembly of notables in each community and village chiefs, who are often only front-men for the wise elders — the ones who take all important decisions in the seclusion of the sacred grove. From the bureaucrats' point of view, it has made the region almost ungovernable.

In 1982, the Casamance independence movement hoisted its flag of rebellion over Government House in Ziguinchor. The rebels under arms may number only a few thousand, but it is generally believed that they command support from a substantial cross-section of their people. In May 1991, after years of sporadic rebel attacks, peace talks with the government produced a ceasefire. Some of the leaders of the Casamance Movement of Democratic Forces (MFDC) came out of hiding, and the government's tacit recognition of them lent weight to the independence cause. A 'peace management committee' was set up, but a radical wing of the MFDC, well armed with kalashnikovs and rocket launchers, promptly split off to continue the armed struggle. With the approach of the 1993 elections, the tempo of attacks and government counter-attacks mounted, leaving several hundred dead in little more than six months.

Few observers believe that the Casamance problem can be resolved by eliminating the relatively small guerrilla movement. Indeed, the separatist movement is likely to be strengthened if the exploratory drilling currently taking place off the Casamance coast finds commercially viable quantities of oil. Some fear that the forces of disintegration might then spread to the Peulh communities of the Fouta Toro — the middle valley of the Senegal River. They, too, complain of the neglect of their needs by a central government which shows little concern for the rural areas.

The only solution in sight is a Commission on Regional Decentralisation, which is not making much progress. Some doubt whether the Wolof who run the country would consider even partial self-government for the Casamance or the Fouta Toro. In the end, however, they may not have much choice.

Mauritanian refugees in the middle

At the other end of the country from the Casamance, in camps strung out along the Senegal River, are the victims of a crisis in Mauritania: 50,000 Mauritanian refugees, whose lives were shattered in 1989 when disputes along the Senegal River border between farmers and Mauritanian herders escalated into serious rioting. Senegalese workers living in the Mauritanian capital of Nouakchott were attacked, which prompted angry Senegalese crowds to harass the well-established Mauritanian community in Dakar, who dominated much of the small-scale trading there and in other towns. Most fled from Senegal, abandoning their homes and businesses.

The government of Mauritania — controlled by 'white' Moors of Arab descent — not content with the exodus of Senegalese nationals from its territory, then expelled tens of thousands of its own black population from their homes, forcing them to seek refuge across the river in Senegal. One camp, at Ndioum, has held nearly 3,000 men, women, and children since they were evicted from their lands in 1989. Even before the crisis, these lands had been coveted by the Moors displaced from their traditional terrain farther north by years of drought. Whole villages were uprooted, and the Ndioum camp is divided into 23 sections, one per village.

The camp coordinator says the UN High Commissioner for Refugees has reduced their monthly food ration from 14 kg each at the beginning to 7.5 kg now. They have organised schooling for their children, but few if any of the adults have been able to find jobs. In response to a UNHCR questionnaire asking whether they want to go home or stay in Senegal., they all replied 'Go home — with conditions'. But their conditions, including restoration of property or compensation, and a total amnesty, are not likely to be acceptable to Mauritania. So the refugees remain in the camps, where many of their children have known no other life.

Children playing with home-made toys in the camp for Mauritanian refugees at Ndioum

BERNARD TAYLOR/OXFAM

The wheels grind slower

IN MANY AREAS of the Senegalese economy, the process of development is shifting into reverse gear. A few years ago Senegal produced shoes, turned out a moderate quantity of galvanised sheet metal, and even had a vehicle-assembly plant. By the end of the 1980s shoe production was down to zero, the car factory had gone, and sheet-metal output was a mere one-sixth of the level ten years earlier.

Is this due to excessively high production costs, prompting firms to move to other countries? Inefficient companies that couldn't cope with outside competition? An inevitable consequence of the economic structural adjustment process? Whatever the analysis, it doesn't alter the fact that industrial output remains the smallest contributor (18 per cent) to the country's income. Figures for 1990 show the primary sector (agriculture, livestock, fisheries)

contributing 20 per cent, and the service sector (trade, transport, communications) a massive 60 per cent.

Production of phosphates — the third-biggest export earner after fish and peanuts — rose fairly steadily during the 1980s, but other industrial output such as salt, cement, and fertiliser showed only a modest improvement.

Senegal has substantial known mineral reserves — high-grade iron ore, copper, chromite, gold, and marble — in its eastern region. But without existing transport facilities from these remote areas, the cost of exploitation at current world prices is judged uneconomic.

One historical cause of Senegal's economic problems was that a wide industrial base was developed during the colonial period, with the aim of serving the whole of French West Africa. Since

BERNARD TAYLOR/OXFAM

The Senegal Sugar Company, an agro-industrial complex on the Senegal River, employs 5,000 workers on its irrigated cane plantations and in its refinery. It produces about 70,000 tons of refined sugar for the domestic market, but its output could be greater.

independence this large market has withered away, as each country has sought to meet its own needs. As a result, many companies found themselves operating far below capacity, with an excessive burden of plant and equipment.

Socialism turned inside-out

The government's New Industrial Policy, launched in 1984 under the structural adjustment regime, aimed to attract new industries to the country, to privatise all activities that could be detached from the public sector, and to lower customs barriers, exposing local producers to the bracing air of foreign competition.

This was a complete about-turn from previous industrial policies, which were based on the protection of local industry and socialist principles of state management. Neither the protection nor the principles had really worked: labour productivity had been declining in most industrial sectors since the mid-1970s; but, as in agriculture, no one was prepared for the sudden change. A further shrinkage in jobs has thus meant a rapid expansion of the informal sector — especially in Dakar and the other main towns — and a rise in urban unemployment.

Educated for unemployment

There were 143,000 people out of work in Dakar alone by 1991 — almost 25 per cent of the active population, according to a recent survey. Nationally, unemployment levels had already reached 20 per cent by 1988. This would be bad enough if the country's workforce was not increasing; in fact, it is estimated that 100,000 young people are entering the job market every year. With recruitment to the public sector virtually frozen and formal jobs in the private sector declining, the chances of finding work are now better for those with less education. Despite the remarkable Senegalese capacity for getting by somehow, this state of affairs poses a serious threat to peace and social stability.

The back-street economy

The 'informal sector' is a dry, academic term to describe the hive of makeshift livelihoods — market traders, artists, hairdressers, transporters, dressmakers, builders and traders of all kinds — which makes life possible for most of the people most of the time. Partly because of this name, the informal sector is usually regarded as subsidiary to the formal economy of 'proper' businesses and jobs. Actually, it's the other way round.

There were about 600,000 people with jobs in the informal sector in the late 1980s, compared with 200,000 in the formal economy. Since then, job losses have pushed the number close to one million.

As businesses and employment have shrunk, so have the government's tax receipts. To make up the deficit, it can choose between taxing the rest more heavily (which could be counterproductive) ... or closing up the sytem's many loop-holes (which would offend many of the government's supporters) ... or finding new sources of revenue. The World Bank suggests finding ways to tax the informal sector. But this could stifle its vitality, or force it further underground.

Pay-offs for some

The government did recently succeed in persuading the World Bank to pay for a voluntary redundancy programme, to slim down the over-staffed civil service. In the first year, the Bank paid for 2,000 redundancies and the payroll dropped accordingly. In the second year, 1,385 took their golden handshake ... but somehow 1,450 others managed to get recruited — which meant a net increase in staff numbers.

The World Bank insists that it is too early to draw conclusions about the New Industrial Policy which it inspired. But in eight years it has produced no signs of an economic upturn. That's not to say that a restructuring of the economy wasn't necessary: almost everyone agrees that it was. But many doubt whether the policy will fulfil its promise of economic growth.

BERNARD TAYLOR/OXFAM

Apprentice mechanics in Dakar, trained by ASAFIN, a local development group. Senegal needs much more of this type of investment.

53

Mbalax for relax

THE OLD MAN on the drum is laying down a throbbing beat, accentuated now and again with a blast on the tin whistle between his teeth. His rhythm underpins an intricate, dancing melody from the one-string calabash instruments played with bows by his two fellow musicians, as they stroll between the tables of a local drinking parlour.

In the back streets of Velingara, away from the narrow streets crowded with shops and stalls and pigs snuffling in the dust, an unmarked gate leads into a compound where, under a pergola of woven mats, a group of townspeople are sitting around, chatting and listening. This is the Casamance, where the popular drink is the local palm wine, home-made and cheap. It's the region which gave birth to the *kora*, a 21-stringed lute which is the typical instrument of West Africa.

Everyone's having a good time, in a setting that's a long way from the kind of arena with spotlights and stereophonic sound where sophisticated singers and musicians are playing the traditional music of Senegal in a modern idiom. The Wolof call it *mbalax*: their special blend of rhythm and relax. Youssou Ndour, whose latest album was nominated for a 1993 Grammy Award as best foreign record, is the 'King of Mbalax'.

For a different kind of relaxation, the Senegalese love their spectator sports. First and foremost is traditional wrestling, which was witnessed in 1795 by the Scottish explorer, Mungo Park, who wrote admiringly of the combatants' dexterity and judgement. A championship match today can carry a purse of £8,000 for the title-holder and half as much for the challenger. Big fights attract up to 50,000 spectators. If the national champion is defeated, it's the talk of Dakar.

Football is also very popular. Children start young, playing on the beach or any patch of open ground, while international matches against other West African teams attract large crowds. The best players have the chance of being signed up to play in European leagues.

Along the Atlantic coast, canoe races in brightly-painted craft are often the focus of festivities, while every day the beaches around Dakar are crowded with keep-fit classes of young people in shorts and t-shirts, and solitary joggers in smart track suits.

Words and pictures

At this westernmost edge of Africa, poised between desert, forests, and ocean, Sahelian life is a rich fabric of many ethnic strands, each with its own distinctive history and culture. What is special about Senegal is its readiness to absorb and adapt the attributes of many diverse cultures. Léopold Senghor, who liked to think of his country as 'the Greece of Africa', was in some ways the archetype of this cosmopolitan outlook, his poetry and political philosophy bridging African and European traditions.

In a more modern idiom, the renowned Senegalese writer and film-maker Sembene Ousmane was one of the first to give African cinema an international audience. Recently, his *Camp de Thiaroye* and *Guelwaar* have won prizes at the Venice Film Festival, and others, such as Djibril Diop and Paulin Vieyra, have also won esteem for Senegal in the film world.

Figurative painting is not an indigenous art form, but a growing number of artists have found new expression for the African visual

Rastafarian singer
Bob Marley,
immortalised in a
'Set Setal' street
mural in Dakar

imagination through an adaptation of European abstract, surreal, or naif styles. Some achieve an original and authentic fusion, for example in fine vignettes of daily life, painted on glass; others are largely a decorative reworking of models from elsewhere.

Not all the cultural influences which Senegal absorbs are wholesome. Imported films and TV programmes purvey seductive images of glamour and violence, with amoral, consumerist attitudes which are at odds with the traditional values of Senegalese life. Material possessions, these soap operas and game shows seem to say to the shanty-town dwellers who crowd into a neighbour's shack to watch TV, are the only measure of earthly salvation.

One original form of street art, deriving inspiration from many sources, burst on the Dakar scene in 1990 as part of a spontaneous city clean-up movement called 'Set Setal' — roughly translatable as 'Clean to be clean' or 'Cleanliness is purity'. This was an impromptu movement of young people, many of them unemployed, to tidy up their neighbourhoods, remove rubbish from the streets, and then beautify the open spaces with trees, flowers, and artworks of their own making. Wood, stones, old car tyres, and paints of every colour were used to make sculpture, brightly-painted monuments, and murals of many kinds. Some were just for fun, but most had a serious message, honouring political and religious leaders and heroes of the struggle against French imperialism, such as Lat-Dyor; others conveyed public-service messages about health, hygiene, and AIDS. Lions and doves of peace were recurrent images in *set setal* — reflections of the young generation's will for power and independence, but without violence.

'Beware of AIDS': a 'Set Setal' mural in Dakar

Sopi! Sopi! Sopi!

EVERYWHERE IN THE TOWNS and the cities of Senegal the rallying cry is change: *Sopi! We want change!* The political opposition has adopted this convenient slogan to declare its rejection of the status quo. But the demand for change is more than a political slogan. It expresses a belief that the whole system of government is deficient and must be reformed.

There are some who believe that a fundamental process of change is already under way in Senegalese society, which President Diouf's recent re-election for a seven-year term can do nothing to check — and which he, to survive, will have to accept. They see the old feudal patterns of power crumbling and a new, hopeful future on the horizon, beginning a moral and spiritual liberation which never came with political independence. For the first 30 years, the government always maintained that political sovereignty was only one step towards the goal of real economic independence. Yet that goal has receded year by year.

There are some new signs of hope on the political and social map of Senegal. It is a fact, for example, that a large proportion of the population was born since independence and is therefore burdened neither by memories of a colonial past nor (perhaps more importantly) by an uncritical acceptance of their own post-independence leadership.

It is also true that, as the authority of central government has been eroded, people have been inventing their own futures and devising their own self-help schemes. The government itself has been obliged to make the institutions of democracy — notably its election procedures — more openly democratic. This, if nothing else, has given people hope that change is possible and cannot be blocked in all circumstances by those in authority.

A rural revival?

At the village level, too, things are changing. More information and ideas are filtering through, to help rural people innovate and improve traditional practices. And more village associations are grouping themselves into federations in order to share their experience and claim some voice in policy-making. The sort of progress that Senegal can be proud of is the success of a public education campaign against bush fires, which laid waste to six million hectares a year in the early 1970s. By 1988, this figure had been cut to 130,000 hectares.

There are some possibilities, at least in theory, of a rural revival. On a small scale, affordable techniques of organic farming are restoring or protecting endangered soils. Much more could be done at low cost to promote these methods. And one study has suggested that agroforestry — mixing trees and crops — could double the number of people able to live in the peanut basin. In one region, the study points out, millet production was doubled in the 1960s by planting 50 *acacia albida* trees per hectare, their leaves giving the land as much natural fertiliser as 50 tons of manure. That's all very well, farmers say, but *acacia* trees take 15 years or more to get established, and many die in times of drought.

Time to start sharing the power

Meanwhile, as some foreign aid agencies and voluntary groups have realised, the essential key to progress for most

Mme Assiata Sy, a leading figure in the development group Maisons Familiales Rurales, in her office near Ndioum. Through the 'associative movement', ordinary Senegalese people are acquiring more control over their own lives.

Senegalese lies in their acquiring more control over their own lives. At the most basic level this is happening with literacy and health campaigns; at an institutional level it is happening with the new growth of village federations and associations of small businesses, which are finding they can have more influence collectively than separately.

But a new culture of self-reliance within Senegal will not be enough to enable the country to fulfil its potential. The international community must take some of its own structural adjustment medicine and start reforming the systems of foreign aid and trade which perpetuate global poverty. The fragmented mini-economies of Africa, lacking a big enough domestic market to provide them with an engine for growth, find themselves being tossed like flimsy *pirogues* in the turbulent wake of the rich world's economic battleships.

The road to regional recovery

For West African countries like Senegal, domestic and international trends all seem to point to deepening dependency on a global economy which is impervious to

their needs. Yet there is still a way out which could, with the necessary vision and leadership, save the day: the path of regional integration. Many efforts to develop this path have been blocked by those with a vested interest in the status quo, but some leading economists of the region now argue that it is the only way to stop the economic slide.

In a recent book, Moustapha Kassé, the Director of Senegal's Centre for Applied Economic Research, argues that 'a wide and deep process of integration would make it possible to resolve the development crisis'. He advocates a regional division of labour, building on each country's strengths and natural endowments, together with a regional system of finance and credit, to establish the best conditions for exploiting all the resources of the sub-region. As things stand, Kassé points out, no individual country has a real chance of recovery on its own.

In fact, Senegal has been at the forefront of efforts to build closer regional cooperation. President Diouf is committed to the idea of a regional parliament, though the government sees many political hurdles in the way of full economic integration. The official view is that a start could be made by developing communication and transport links, and coordinating policies on information, health, education, and the environment.

Senegal has direct experience of this from its short-lived union with the Gambia in the Confederation of Senegambia. Created in 1982, the Confederation was fairly limited in scope and, after some friction between the two countries, President Diouf abandoned it in 1989 as 'a waste of time and money'.

A new start for Senegal

In some respects, Senegal is a microcosm of the crises afflicting Africa at the end of the twentieth century. Many of the problems are complex, and the solutions tried so far have had meagre success. At the same time, it's just possible that — given the right push from within and without — this country could become a beacon to guide others towards an authentically African way of development before the continent's nation states are 100 years old. It would be a huge achievement, considering how little they had to start with and how much has been stacked against them. But for that to be feasible, much more will have to change.

The optimistic view is that after a mere generation of independence, Senegal — and much of Africa besides — is already shaking off some of the shackles it inherited, and others that its leaders had imposed on their people. In historical terms, thirty years is not long for a new nation to find its feet.

Unless one can identify the pebble that starts a landslide, it is never easy to pinpoint the moment when a nation embarks on a process of change and renewal. But for the people of Senegal, it has to happen sooner, rather than later.

'What future for the youth of Senegal?', asks a street mural in Dakar

Facts and figures

Baobab tree

Land area: 197,000 sq km

Population (1993 estimate): 8 million

Annual population growth (1990-2000 estimate): 2.8%

Life expectancy at birth: 48 years

Main urban centres: Dakar region (pop. 2 million), Thiès (319,000), Kaolack (181,000), St Louis (179,000)

Principal ethnic groups: Wolof, Serer, Peulh, Toucouleur, Diola

Languages: Wolof, Pulaar, and other national languages. Official language (understood by approximately 20%): French

Adult literacy: 38%

GDP per capita (1992): £440 (equivalent to approximately £250 at 1994 exchange rates)

Annual growth of GNP (average for 1980-90): 0%

Nutrition: Daily calorie supply per person, as percentage of requirements: 84%

Health: Percentage of population with access to safe water: urban 79%, rural 38%

Currency: 1 Franc CFA = 1 centime (under a fixed exchange rate, 100 FCFA = 1 French franc)

Main agricultural production: peanuts, millet, sorghum, manioc, rice, cotton, livestock

Principal exports: fish and fish products, peanut products, phosphates, chemicals

Foreign debt (1992): US$3.6 billion

Dates and events

11th century AD: Arrival of Islam with the conquering Almoravids from North Africa.

12th century: Founding of the Kingdom of Djoloff.

15th century: Arrival of the first Portuguese explorers.

1588-1677: The Dutch establish fortified trading posts along the Senegal coast.

1659: Fort of St Louis founded and named in honour of Louis XIII of France.

1677-1815: The French and English compete for control of the island of Gorée and coastal trade.

1815: Treaties of Paris and Vienna give France control of the Senegal coast, and ban the slave trade.

1854: France begins to colonise the Senegalese mainland.

1876: Resistance leader Lat-Dyor is killed. The coastal region is annexed by the French. Dakar-St Louis railway constructed.

1871-80: Policy of 'assimilation' grants French citizenship to inhabitants of St Louis, Dakar, Gorée, and Rufisque, with the right to elect Deputies to the French National Assembly.

1904: Present boundaries of Senegal established.

1914-18: More than 200,000 men from France's African territories are enlisted to fight in World War I.

1957: France moves to split up its West African colony into small separate states. The future President, Léopold Senghor, objects to this 'balkanisation'.

1960: In June, Senegal achieves independence in federation with Mali. The

Pekesse: recycling old rope from discarded fishing nets

federation breaks up and in September the Republic of Senegal is proclaimed.

1962: Political crisis, following which the Prime Minister, Mamadou Dia, is condemned to a long prison sentence.

1966: Senegal becomes effectively a one-party state.

1968: Start of long and devastating drought; great damage to livestock and crops through much of 1970s and 1980s.

1974: A second political party, the Parti Democratique Sénégalais (PDS), led by Maître Abdoulaye Wade, is granted recognition.

1975: Mamadou Dia is freed in a general amnesty: Senegal now one of the few African countries without political prisoners.

1976: Constitutional change allows formation of a third political party, the leftist Parti Africain de l'Indépendance (PAI).

1978: Three parties contest Presidential and legislative elections. Senghor is re-elected.

1980: President Senghor retires to make way for Abdou Diouf.

1981: Creation of Confederation of Senegambia. President Diouf amends constitution to abolish restrictions on formation of political parties.

1983: Diouf wins popular endorsement in elections.

1988: The Socialist Party of President Diouf wins 103 of 120 seats in general election, setting off violent demonstrations against alleged vote-rigging.

1989: Conflict with Mauritania. More than 60,000 Mauritanians deported to Senegal.

1993: President Diouf re-elected for seven-year term.

1994: The Communauté Financière Africaine (CFA) Franc is devalued in January by 50 per cent. (Since 1948 it had been worth 50 to the French Franc.)

Sources and further reading

Club du Sahel (1988), *The Sahel Facing the Future*, Paris: OECD.

Cross, Nigel and Rhiannon Barker (1992), *At the Desert's Edge*, London: Panos Publications.

Cruise O'Brien, Donal (1971), *The Mourides of Senegal*, Oxford: Clarendon Press.

Diallo, Mamadou (ed.) (1989), *Le Sénégal: géographie physique, humaine, économique*, Paris: EDICEF.

Diop, Momar Coumba (ed.) (1992), *Sénégal: trajectoires d'un Etat*, Dakar/Paris: CODESRIA, Karthala.

Dumont, René (1986), *Pour l'Afrique, j'accuse*, Paris: Plon.

Kane, Karamoko (1993), 'Senegal', in *The Impact of Structural Adjustment on the Population of Africa* (Aderanti Adepoju, ed.), London: UNFPA/James Currey.

Kassé, Moustapha (1991), *Le développement par l'intégration*, Dakar: Nouvelles Editions Africaines du Sénégal.

Ki-Zerbo, Joseph (1978), *Histoire de l'Afrique noire*, Paris: Hatier.

Ndione, Emmanuel et al. (1992), *La ressource humaine: avenir des terroirs*, Dakar: ENDA.

Organisation for African Unity (1992), *Africa's Children, Africa's Future: Human Investment Priorities for the 1990s*, Dakar: OAU/UNICEF.

Ousmane, Sembene (1970), *God's Bits of Wood*, London: Heinemann.

Saglio, Christian (1980), *Sénégal*, Paris: Seuil.

Schoonmaker Freudenberger, Karen (1991), *Mbegué: The Disingenuous Destruction of a Sahelian Forest*, London: IIED Drylands Issues Paper.

Sweeney, Philip (ed.) (1990), *The Gambia and Senegal*, Insight Guide, London: APA Publications.

Sylla, Assane (1992), *Le Peuple Lébou*, Dakar: NEAS.

Toupet, Charles (1992), *Le Sahel*, Paris: Nathan.

Touré, Oussouby (1990), *Where Herders Don't Herd Any More: Experience from the Ferlo, Northern Senegal*, London: IIED Drylands Issues Paper.

World Bank (1987), *Senegal: An Economy under Adjustment*, Washington: World Bank

World Bank (1992), *Rapport d'Actualisation Macroeconomique*, Washington, World Bank.

Acknowledgements

Many people helped in the preparation of this book. For the benefit of their ideas, experience, and practical guidance, the author particularly wishes to thank Thandika Mkandawire, Jacques Bugnicourt, Bara Gueye, Ousmane Sow, and the Oxfam-Dakar team.

Oxfam in Senegal

MANY OF THE PROJECTS featured in this book are supported by Oxfam (UK and Ireland). In Senegal, ordinary people are free to form groups to improve their own living conditions, and to campaign for a fair share of the nation's resources. But poor communities often lack the necessary information and organisational skills to get things changed. So Oxfam's funding always has two aims: to bring practical benefits, such as clean drinking water or veterinary training — but also to strengthen community groups, helping them to identify their own problems, work out their own solutions, and get organised to manage their own lives.

In the year ended April 1994, Oxfam spent over £400,000 in Senegal, helping to develop village federations such as **ADENA**, networks of urban women's groups such as **PROFEMU**, and local non-governmental organisations such as **Maisons Familialies Rurales**. Oxfam often takes risks and funds new grassroots initiatives which might not attract funds from other agencies. But all the groups that Oxfam supports must be democratically constituted, and able to manage their own affairs and represent the interests of their members and the neighbouring population. Projects are not funded if they are likely to make women's lives harder, or to damage the natural environment. The emphasis of Oxfam's programme is to help poor communities achieve positive change in their lives, through communal organisation and concerted action.

The well at Tekkangel village, Ferlo region

JEREMY HARTLEY/OXFAM